The Success Factor

Our Work Matters

NIKKI FLOWERS

Contents

Visit Nikki Flowers's Website for the latest news and updates.

Website: emotionalfictionpublications.com

Instagram:
instagram.com/the_emotional_connect

Emotional Fiction Publishing Instagram:
instagram.com/emotionalfictionpublishing

Twitter: @NikkiFlowers_1

Facebook:
facebook.com/EmotionalFictionPublishingHouse

Dedication

I would like to dedicate this self-help journey to all the women and men who are going through the emotions of life, their own personal struggles, and are at a crossroads between doing what is right and what is wrong.

Everyone must walk into their journey of life to find their purpose. This book is just a little inspiration to get you going. The two poems provided in this book, come straight from behind the prison walls. Prison Minds "do" read…Freedom Writers of the City. The two poems are Daydreams

By: Remy Stover and What More Can I Say By:
Mark Bunting

I would like to thank Remy Stover & Mark
Bunting for allowing me to showcase their
emotional talent. Remember what I said to the both
of you—if you can put all that energy into doing the
wrong thing, just imagine how great you would be
if you played by the rules.

I want to thank God for ordaining my steps to
becoming a better person and a pillar in my
community.

I would also like to thank everyone who has
supported me from the beginning.

For everyone that picks up this book, for
whatever reason, please take the time to nurture
your purpose. Everything you want to accomplish is
possible through prayer and hard work.

Being Nikki Flowers

On June 25, 2007, I was sentenced to serve five years in a State Correctional Facility, due to selling narcotics in my community. Everything in my life as I knew it would soon change as my life was spared through incarceration. If I had not gone to prison, I would not be able to share my story with you today because I would be dead. Prison saved me from myself in a way. I had to go through everything I had to at that point for me to get to this moment right here, right now. I now realize that my journey is a blessing to myself and others.

Through God placing me in a situation where I had no choice but to be still and evaluate my choices, I was able to walk into my purpose. Instead of the destructive path I was on, I became a writer, a self-published author, and a boss. Every negative thought and feeling I had ever had about myself, and others, I took it out on the paper I purchased through commissary. In nine months', time I birthed my first book, which also happened to be the start to the renewal of my mind. My whole life I had blamed others for the choices I made. I did not see anything wrong with what I was doing to myself, to my family, or to my community—until I was placed in a controlled environment.

In those five years I was incarcerated, I was forced to become clean of all the toxins I had exposed my body to, while learning a lot about myself, others, and how to take responsibility for my own thoughts, feelings and actions. Writing my first four novels while incarcerated, I found my therapy, which taught me that I could do something besides sell narcotics. I created my own lane and healing process with my genre, Emotional Fiction. The best definition of which is 'Reality Urban Fiction wrapped in a beautiful lie.' Taking real life issues, I had been in throughout my life I took this motto and tailored it to fit me.

Today, December 13, 2017, ten and a half years later, I've realized how showing my scars has helped others, how my life experiences gave me the creditability to help the next incarcerated person change their life—for the better. I now work in the same county jail that I once wore 'reds', serving my sentence, in order to give back to my community for all of the lives that I had ruined through my own personal destruction.

Even through all the ups and downs I can honestly say the best feeling in the world is knowing that there are people who Google me, Nikki Flowers, for words of encouragement, publishing advice, to share their testimony, and to purchase my novels.

Emotional Fiction Publishing

Emotional Fiction Publishing was established on November 9, 2016. The publishing firm is geared toward self-motivation, positivity from within, and empowerment for the imprisoned that have no voice.

Through the publishing firm, incarcerated prisoners can self-publish their bodies of work within the following categories: short stories, collaborations, which means taking two categories to create your own genre, poetry, self-help, educational, nonfiction, and emotional fiction manuscripts.

Emotional fiction was created within an imprisoned mind with nothing more than a notebook, a pen, and a dream.

General Submissions

Urban 'Emotional' Fiction (Street Lit), can be submitted by all writers who are willing to work hard at becoming their own boss, a best-selling, self-published author, and are motivated in developing a successful brand. The publishing firm is geared towards helping the writer in you become great, so that you can find the boss within you, while creating your own lane.

All you need is a finished manuscript to get started right now. Do not put it off. Explore

Emotional Fiction Publishing Firm right now—I mean it, push that button right now to explore at *www.emotionalfictionpublishingfirm.com* and get all of the information you need. *You never know what you are capable of doing if you do not try.* Submit an online outline today!

Please keep in mind that if a manuscript is being considered a follow up email will be sent out to notify you.

Day Dreams

By: Remy Stover

I've been wide-awake, dreaming of stars and moons, space and cosmic bliss.

Dare to dream, Pisces of the stars, moon, and rivers of cosmic fish.

Seemingly true, a lesson for youth, you're damned if you do and damned if you don't. But I will be damned if I let you, and be God damned if I won't.

Metaphorically, under the weight of the world, my knees have literally buckled,

They throw you away, give a fuck what you say, and conclude that he has been troubled.

I'm sick of the hate, I'm sick of the crime, I'm sick of the law, I'm sick of it all. I'm sick of the reds, I'm sick in the head, I keep coming back, I'm thick in the skull.

I'm sick for the kids with nowhere to live, I'm sick of the rich, with nothing to do but bitch, I'm sick for the poor, I'm sick for the whores who fuck just to get a hit, a junkie ass fix, I'm sick of the men who act sick with these women and leave them stuck with a baby while they hustle is booming.

You slid out of sight, let him hit the first night, but want to be treated as ladies. Come the fuck on… Yeah right!

I'm sick for the vets who wake up in sweats, when sleep should be at peace. The best of the best, toughest of tough, in a corner while he weeps.

I've been wide-awake dreaming of stars and moons, space and cosmic bliss.

Dare to dream Pisces of the stars, moon, rivers of cosmic fish.

Seemingly true, lesson for youth, you're damned if you do and damned if you don't. But I'll be damned if I let you, and be God damned if I won't.

Simplistic beauty streaks the faces of the tired and the weak, murder's a sin but it's poetic when you'd kill to be free.

Some kill for money, some kill for God, but most kill for greed. Some kill for pride, some kill to thrive; I'd just kill to be me.

Either ride the wave or turn the page, eventually all will end.

Remember a time when we were just nine and scared to make new friends, I've been wide-awake dreaming of stars and moon, space and cosmic bliss.

Dare to dream Pisces of the stars, moon, and rivers of cosmic fish.

Seemingly true, a lesson for youth, you're damned if you do and damned if you don't. But I will be damned if I let you, and be God damned if I won't.

Now Let's Get Started

INTRODUCTION

As believers in ourselves, and our storytelling abilities, the soul, which is composed of intellect and will, will always tell your truth. Will and our emotions must be free and truthful within ourselves. This is a must if you want your dreams to become goals, your goals to become reality and your reality to be executed.

Being in a healthy thinking process is an escape, the therapeutic essence of the perfectionism we seek through creating goals and completing them is much needed to define our definition of success. This guide is an outlet to articulate what you are experiencing—what you are seeing through your eyes while trying to be the best _**YOU**_, you can be. Whether it is love, happiness, anger, or sadness; if lost or on point, the key to being successful is never giving up when life shows up. When this on key factor is mastered creating a moment of clarity you will be successful at heart.

This book is not just about writing down goals, attempting to complete them, giving you a life lesson or trying to sell you a gimmick. It's a tool to dig deeper within yourself and the talent God gave you, to emerge with the good fortunes of knowledge and insight hidden behind boundaries. The freedom to express your emotions and sick thinking with the insight that comes from the heart of one's self, and trusting the creative beast within you, yourself to be great at the talent God gave you.

Becoming a great _**YOU**_, finding your truth serum and connecting others' hearts and minds with a reflection of your definition of success is what this book is about. Teaching the inner strength of what you can provide to the world for you, **YOUSELF** to be successful and others who follow.

Do you have what it takes to be successful? You will find out while challenging yourself to discover your own unique allegories and those diamonds in the rough that make you who you are.

AMBITION

(Step One)

___AMBITION-___ the determination to succeed.

This is where your dreams become reality as you begin to shape and form them without any doubts.

Though an army may encamp against me, my heart shall not fear; through war may rise against me, in this I will be confident.

Psalms 27:3

As people, we are in a constant frame of change and often don't realize it. My ambitions are not the same today as they were yesterday. How about you?

___CONFIDENCE-___ feeling of reliance or certainty; sense of self-reliance; boldness.

You need confidence within yourself, your craft, and your writing capabilities for ambition to play its part. Confidence plants the seed, while ambition waters the idea until deeply rooted and planned accordingly within a rough outline.

MATURITY- the state, fact, or period of being mature.

Maturity of one's ideas can build confidence and ambition within your writing. We all must start somewhere—focus on one idea at a time, one word at a time, one sentence at a time, and one chapter at a time by putting your thoughts, which are running rampant in your mind, on paper for about an hour.

Some people are naturally driven with confidence and ambition; however, we are all not constructed the same. Sometimes you need a push in the right direction and here it is.

Me, personally, it took me twenty-nine years of my life to gain confidence—to appreciate myself and believe that I could do something positive in my life. It took twenty-nine years for me to stop being a nuisance in my community, pick up an ink pen and find the words to mate with my pieces of paper. My success was waiting on me inside of a blank notebook. It was just that simple once I sat still long enough to figure it out. What is it that **_YOU_** are good at?

MATE- come or bring together for marriage or breeding.

There are five different definitions for the word mate, but the brief description above created my first successful thought. On August 23, 2007, I took to the idea of being the voice of no reasoning and created my own lane with the talent God had given me. I had been up-state, away from family for exactly a month. Being incarcerated in prison doing a five-year sentence I had a lot of anger inside me and I needed to get it out. Thankfully, while sitting in county jail I was introduced to urban literature for the first time and I fell in love with the essence of the storyline and how it resembled my life. From that moment on, I knew I was going to start writing a masterpiece.

I had read a book or two in my time. Books like Super Head's, *Taking Down the Industry*, 50 Cent's, *Bulletproof Story*, and L.L. Cool J's, *I Make My Own Rules*; I had read each of them from the front to the back. Even though I had read them from front to back, I had never stayed up into the wee hours of the morning reading—that was until someone slid an urban fiction book under my jail cell door.

I can still remember looking at the book and turning my nose up at it. Eventually, I became bored within the small space I was sharing, and I needed something to do. My negative energy had taken over my thoughts and my significant other was a constant reminder of the bad choices I had made. Angry, I pick up the book and I read the cover. *What the heck? You don't have anything else better to do. Read it.*

First chapter in and I was going, going, gone. I could relate to the narcotics, the danger, the lovemaking, and the unspoken messages of life in the neighborhoods of America. That night I learned that regular people like you and me knew how to create one heck of a story. Not just a story about how they made stupid decisions after stardom, but a story about reality. I was hooked to everything written on those pages; I was reading my life's story.

Being fueled by negativity from so many failed relationships my thoughts began to trip over one another. Suddenly, I had an epiphany—God had had enough of me. My confidence and ambition aligned at that very moment as I reached the end of the book. In the coming days, weeks, months and years, my ambition and determination to succeed would be the greatest comeback I would have. My confidence would be the uppercut sliding through, connecting with the jaws of everyone that said I would never amount to anything. The ambition of a rider was born instantly.

I remember it like it was yesterday—I picked up the $0.40 pen and began to bleed out my cries on a $1.37 commissary notebook with nothing more than a mere thought. It was not long before I took that thought and made it tangible. Taking one word I turned it into one long run-on sentence that collaborated into chapters.

In that short time my hand and pen had become soul mates, bringing to life every thought I had conjured up and putting it on paper. The words continued falling in love, bringing forth a marriage–

–breeding a new genre of life into me. In the next breath I saw that God had provided me a finished product. My completed novel, Twist of Fate was born just nine months later. For me, at that time, my pen and paper told my truth, my love, my happiness, my sorrow, my lies and what I wanted to be, as well as who I was.

I found myself breaking within the closed-in cell walls and I needed a way out. I made up my mind…I was going to change the game in Urban Literature. Thankfully, the universe sided with me and gave me a moment of clarity. It was entirely up to me to water the seed that had been planted and to give myself a chance. It was time to do something right for once in my life. I had a story to tell and I wanted everyone to hear me. I was going to be somebody… You are going to be somebody too!

"At that moment of commitment the entire universe conspires to assist you."
J.W. Von Goethe

No matter what happened during my day, my ink pen always mated with my paper. Each day I went back over my thoughts I had written down and my confidence began to grow. It set my soul on fire and all I wanted to do was write—to become a better writer and a published author. In chapter one you must figure out what sets your soul on fire. What's your burning desire? What makes you itch? What is it that drives you to want to succeed in life? Here is where you find out what talent God gave you. In other words, your moment of clarity, **_YOU_** walking into your purpose. We all have struggles, but you cannot let them define you. The moment you do you have lost the battle. When you know, better it is your duty to do better. Do not let your silence enslave you. Allow it to make you strong so that you can have a story to tell. You never know, your struggle can be your success and the road that will lead to helping others. That exactly what I am doing here preaching to **_YOU._** Take an hour out from reading. Think, I mean really think about how you can be successful. Write down 15 things that you are good at. Include what you want to be, what you need to be and how you can help others.

15 Ways to Succeed

1.

2.

3.

4.

5.

6.

7.

8.

9.

10.

11.

12.

13.

14.

15.

Now that we have determined fifteen different ways on how we can succeed in life we have to set up a plan to get us there. The ambition is flowing through our veins ready to be creative and spontaneous on how we will achieve. No road is to narrow or too long to be conquered.

When you look at yourself in the mirror, what is your definition of success?

*Success-*______________________________

My mother's definition of success was not having to count pennies to pay for her groceries. She worked every day for thirty-three years for *The Board of Education.* It took her until she was sixty-nine years old to catch her first flight and believe in herself enough to start her own business. A year later she died a six-figure earner. When you look at yourself in the mirror are you afraid to take a risk? What is your definition of afraid? What is your definition of risk? I do not want you to write down the dictionary version. Write down what it means to you!

*Afraid-*______________________________________

*Risk-*____

I was a confused alcoholic by thirteen years old, branded with other people's pain because I did not know who I was! At first, I was fueled by the hate I had in my heart for a lot of different reasons. I was in love with my own pain and could not escape it no matter where I went. Since I could not run from myself, I carried the hurt and pain like it was a badge of honor. I did not like the person I was when I looked in the mirror. I could not look at my reflection in the mirror without hanging my head. What I did not know was that the pain I was caring around would soon become a malignant cancer, killing everything good trying to happen in my life until I was thrown in a locked cell.

Taking out my frustrations on life, I had to do something different. I now had a son the same age I was when I was afraid to look in the mirror. He was thirteen left to fend for himself with a mother nowhere to be found. We all have that teachable moment and mine was prison. The pain in my mother's eyes and my son I wanted to be better. I wanted to be successful without having to step on someone else's pain to do so. I went from a prison cell to a CEO of not just one but two businesses. I did not understand my mother's definition of success because it was such a small request all of those years ago when she shared that with me. However, today I get it because many folks cannot pay for their groceries at all. The first step to being successful is being ambitious. Are you ready to work!?!?!

SUCCESS TIP

Everyday read over your fifteen ways that you want to be successful. Make sure you are reading and researching your topics. The more you know the better you are at creating success goals to get you to your goal. Be productive every day! It takes longer to heat up the brain and get the creative juices flowing when the success tools are not being used daily. It is very easy to get cold and fall into a slump when things are not going your way so stay encouraged by creating realistic goals. Remember you must work to get a million dollars and it does not happen over-night. This will keep your ambition intact—you will continue to build confidence and your brand that you have chosen.

SUCCESS TIP

If you wake up and work, study, workout or meditate every day for thirty days, studies have shown it will form a habit. These are the positive habits we need within us to create greatness. Not just in our success themes, but within our daily activities. When you have discipline and positive habits within your daily routine, everything else will eventually fall into place.

<u>DISCIPLINE</u>- training that corrects, molds, or perfects the mental faculties or moral character.

When you find out what you are made of your confidence will be the billboard of success. To build confidence you must take chances and make some mistakes along the way. Just remember, mistakes do not define you—the way you make your comeback will. I cannot stress this point enough, you must write that word, create that sentence, and complete your first draft before becoming the great story.

Most of us out here trying to get our slice of the American pie have full time jobs, are full time students, have families, and a lot more responsibilities where those come from. So—**SET**

UP A SCHEDULE AROUND YOUR DAILY ROUTINE TO WORK ON YOUR SUCCESS.

Most of us are family orientated. We have children to cook and clean up after, we have school and life that shows up no matter what the age is, however, do not use your routine as a crutch. Create a daily planner on an erase board and hang it from the fridge. Change up your daily routine when necessary, and always be proactive when feeling inspired. From here on out, always keep a small notepad and pen in your pocket. This is so you can write down ideas that pop into your head. It may also be used to work on ideas when you have idle time on your hands. Nowadays folks have strayed away from the pen and pad because it has been built into our devices. Nonetheless, for the old school flocks who like carrying around the pencil and paper I do as well.

I am currently working a full-time job, I am promoting my books, and I am running a publishing company and travel agency. I am also a mother, and my better half demands a lot of my attention. Today, I create time where there is no time. I keep an email copy of all projects I'm working on at the time so I can access them at both of my work stations, on my cell phone, and on my lap-top, which I always keep in my vehicle.

Before I tap into my social media, I immediately pull up a writing project to work on, in order to do something productive to help get me closer to a writing goal I have set in place.

Set up the time and place; make time when you do not have the time and be your own boss! If you can get up and punch the clock at your job for someone who is already a millionaire, then you can take the time out of your day to groom yourself in order to become the next one.

Nurture your craft and your beast to give yourself the opportunity to be great and find the boss in **_YOU_**. YOU'RE the most important part of your life. Nobody can care more about your life than you do…

I am in it to win it and to be an expert in the lanes I created for myself. I do not pray for zeros; I pray for commas. The steps in my journey are preordained with blessings. To be or not to be I am blessed, and I will stay blessed for the simple fact that I always bless others.

SUCCESS TIP

Follow your dreams and just do it. Yes, just do it like the Nike slogan says. Believe in your ideas and be the best. Make lots of lists and keep setting yourself up with new challenges. When it starts to rain and believe me it will, don't give up! Don't Give Up! Don't Give Up! Always have fun and look after your team that is there to support you and your dreams. Remember, make a positive difference, and do some good. The more people you bless along the way the better the blessings.

GOALS

(Step Two)

GOALS- the object of a person's ambition or effort; an aim or desired result.

A wise man once said, 'It's far easier to hit a target you can see than to hit one you cannot.'

Okay, you want to know what goals have to do with being successful?

When figuring out what you want to do to be successful, you must be ready to maximize your time and execute your plan. Everyone reading this should have the same idea. Which is to be successful. How do you complete the plan? By creating small tasks to accomplish throughout your productive day until your success story is complete. These are *Goals*.

Goals are another tool you will use in your daily routine. It doesn't matter if you're writing, planning your vacation, putting together your work week, or planning the next steps to have a baby—there is always a goal to be reached. Yes, this is a routine, but what did I say about routines? If you give them thirty days, it will become a habit.

When you pick up the pen to start writing or sit down at your laptop to type, the first thing you have on your mind is doubt. Those small questions begin to nag in the back of your mind. *How will I ever become a six-figure earner? Am I going to make it? Where do I start?* And the list goes on and on and on.

SUCCESS TIP

You can't let doubt interfere with your vision or the desire to create a plan to finish your goals. Without a plan it can become an impossible mission. Creating small goals throughout your learning process to master your craft will help you stay focused and on task.

**VISION-** Act or faculty of seeing; thing or person seen in a dream or trance; mental pictures; imaginative insight; foresight, beautiful person; etc.

All five of these definitions pertain to you. There is a natural ability that grows within you when you're from the streets, living in an urban neighborhood or rural area. Everyone has a different perception of life and your vision must be brought to life.

Right now, you can see the dream, the finished product and your success story taking off. Often, we stare beyond the pen and paper or the laptop, in a trance about the finished project, which has a cumulative of one word—'Goals'. The mental picture is embedded beneath the closed eyelids of every inspired, entrepreneur and that's all right. Your imaginative insight causes you to go hard on preparation for goals and setting up action plays to carry out specific duties. Remember playing video games when you were younger? You start at level one and its easy but the further you go the harder it gets... The same rules apply right here! Nobody cares about your success story more than you do.

When I picked up the pen and paper all I had was a GOAL. At that time, I had no knowledge on what to do and how to begin. A female who resided in a nearby cell was on the same mission as myself and I didn't even know it. I only found out when testing my dreams on another human being that the goal was touchable. I needed some truth and feedback about what was going to happen next in my life. I needed to hear from someone that my goal was obtainable.

A game of one-on-one basketball on a hot summer day cured my curiosity. On the basketball court in Muncy Correctional State Penitentiary my outlook on life was changed in an instant. It was then that I realized all things are possible—even when incarcerated. You see, God suddenly prepared me for what I just asked aloud—he prepared me for my first step, placing me in a conversation with the young lady who resembled me. Talking about the books we'd already read broke the ice as we chucked the basketball at the hoop. One conversation led to another and before long I realized that the charges, we were convicted left us with something in common. Before I knew it, the female confided in me she had started writing a book as well. She had already written four chapters of her own truth and I desperately wanted her to share them with me. When I told her that I was going to pen my first novel she nodded, confirming with confidence that writing a book was tangible. At that moment I had created my first goal.

Talking with her let it be known that my goal was obtainable. And since she looked like me and talked like me, I figured I could write like her—maybe even better. She was the first run in I had had that gave me the strength to want to write. She gave me that push which introduced me to the *confidence* that was much needed.

In the coming chapters I will continue to speak on confidence because you will need it throughout your journey of creating your own lane and success story. Believe me when I say, believing in yourself is a must. No one will believe in you if you do not believe in yourself. You must be your own biggest fan. Strength, courage, vision, and confidence; you will need these traits in every step of your journey.

The woman I had spoken with was another black woman, whose situation was similar to mine——we had both had the same run ins with the law…in other words being a nuisance in our communities.

We were two caged birds trying to sing, trying to find ourselves in a prison in America. When the opportunity finally presented itself, I spoke to her, sharing my ambition, to which she willingly shared her own ambition, allowing me to read the first four chapters of her book. On the commissary paper her words were printed perfectly. Her story flowed and as I read, her words coming to an end, I found myself desperately wanting more. I ran into my next goal, I could feel it, I was on my way to greatness.

Look back on your own journey. Do you see where you've already accomplished goals you had no idea you set in place? Can you see the growth from when you first set out to become your own success story? You are one step closer while reading the self-help guide you have in your hands. Congratulations!

SUCCESS TIP

Goals create excellent opportunities to build self-confidence. Creating small goals and accomplishing them will keep you headstrong. Throughout your journey, you will continue to set small success goals to see just how good you are at the talent given to you.

Small Goals get you going. Make sure to set two a week. Your first goal will be success building oriented and the other will be life structural.

Unbeknownst to one another, we find confidence in relatable people. As I needed to see, her writing to assure myself that writing an urban novel could in fact be done. She needed to hear me tell her that it was a great read. I could not wait to see finished. In that moment, we needed to touch each other's vision to reassure ourselves that the goal was obtainable. When you surround yourself with like-minded people the conversation at the table is totally different. No one is talking about another person; the only discussion is how to be great.

Walking into your purpose can done if you are determined to do so. You can touch your vision through these chapters because writing your own history is just that, your own story. The lane you create today can be the road paved for the next generation of wealth. You are in control; adapt your own success teaching styles and theories until its tangible evidence. For now, I will set three small goals for you to begin working on during your journey to becoming goal oriented.

- **Step One:** Take an hour out of each day to daydream about your definition of success.
- **Step Two:** Research every day! Even when you do not feel like it, you must be proactive within the goals you have created to becoming successful.

- **Step Three:** Read and educate yourself with at least one chapter of a self-help book written by someone who has already made millions of dollars. I promise you this, the goals you read in this book will be the same rules you read in others. At the end of the day, it is the hard work and the never giving up that survives.

After establishing your goals, you must now create a plan to make those goals happen. The tried and true **SMART** acronym is another tool to use to achieve your goals. The acronym definitions are as follows:

S: Specific-Think about the goal you want to achieve. What are trying to accomplish? Why is this goal important? Which resources or limits are involved? This is where you need to be very clear and specific.

M: Measurable-How can you track your progress? Tracking progress keeps you focused and geared up to meet deadlines.

A: Achievable-Stretch your abilities but remain possible. If it help, break the goal into smaller steps. Include potential constraints such as financial factors.

R: Relevant-This step is about ensuring that your goal is important and what you are passionate about. Ask yourself a few of these questions, Does this seem worthwhile? Does this goal align with my other goals?

T: Time-bound-Set a target date. This will prevent everyday life from being the priority and creating excuses that will deter you from achieving your goal.

The SMART plan has come to mean many different things to many different individuals. Keep the focus and motivation at an all-time high. Carve out time to evaluate, review and refocus.

DESTINATION- a place a person is bound for.

SUCCESS TIP

Goals and destination go hand and hand. The goal is where you start, and the destination is the completed goal. When you commit yourself to a specific goal by following through to its destination you certify your aptitude and expand your self-confidence once again. As your self-assurance increases, so does the fight within yourself to create more challenging goals to succeed. Remember, you only succeed when you do not quit. You can only assess what you have done. Once again, practice persistence in everything that you do, and it will become a habit within any goal you need to complete to become a success story. Our Works Matter! The harder you work today will determine when you get to see the back of your eye lid, in other words sleep...

GOAL-ORIENTED- a person's attitude or adjustment revolving around their ambitions.

Become goal-oriented in as many areas of your life that you can. As your goals reach their destination you will grow and progress towards the vision of completing your success story. You will also have a life testimony to tell if you implement the goals in your life and daily activities. When there are no goals to be systematically achieved your business cannot thrive. It will not exist because it will not be finished.

THREE BASIC GOAL TYPES

Immediate Goals: the short goals you completed expeditiously. Immediate goals can be completed in a day or so, or within a period of two months (1-60 days).

<u>EXAMPLE</u>

Aug. 23, 2019

One hour a day for seven days I will do research on the next steps I need to take to be successful. Doing this one goal for two weeks in a row can be the push you need to reach your vision. It has scientifically proven that creating small goals will inspire you to want to work harder. When you overlook what you have accomplished in those two weeks, you will be ready to approach your next goal headstrong. Your destination is the confidence booster.

Intermediate Goals: are goals between immediate and long-range goals. These goals command considerable planning to reach their destination. What will it take to reach these goals? It takes a series of plans and immediate goals to accomplish an intermediate goal. Intermediate goals may be completed in three to six months (90-120 days).

EXAMPLE

Aug. 23, 2019

One hour a day will be spent researching how to guides to be successful.

- Go to your Public Library to read further on business building. Put your phone on silent and in your pocket. Focus!

- Go online and research business strategies on how to become successful when your home. Focus!

Sept. 23, 2019

I will study and write one 60 second pitch a week.

- Set an alarm at 6AM to write thirty minutes before starting your day.

- Read over what was written in the morning and write for thirty minutes before bed.

Oct. 23, 2019

Start researching how to be successful within your dream.

- Research online what needs to be done to be successful within your business structure.

- Research social media sites to see who is in your lane. By doing this you can see what has been done before and what you can do to contribute.

Three immediate goals that reach their destination create an intermediate goal! You expand your self-confidence once again and cannot wait to be creative within the lane you are creating. The best feeling in the world is when you can sit down and see your goals taking action by the hard work you have done.

Long-Range Goals: these goals are your future in the making. Your vision depends upon you reaching your long-range goals and executing them. Your long-range goals consist of the many immediate and intermediate goals you reached with great accomplishment. Your determination and goal setting has finally brought you through to a finished novel.

SUCCESS TIP

Following your dreams should not take up your free time it should fill it. Long-range goals can expand over a lifetime; however, I suggest you keep them within a twelve-month timeline when it comes to completing your determination plans to be successful. Anything over a year and you are not executing your immediate goals to get you one-step closer to your dreams. This can depend on what your definition of success is also. It can take years for you to build an empire and sometimes it will take longer for you to execute certain goals. You must constantly push yourself, creating new goals to accomplish, in order to become great. Stay on your path of greatness. Remember this, different success stories require different goals and time frames.

Allow yourself to be great! For me, having experience with setting and executing goals, I know that if I set goals every day and execute them in a timely manner, I can write a novel within a three-month timeframe.

I finished my first novel in nine months. I did not know it was going to be finished in nine months until I understood its purpose. It was the start of my process of becoming successful. In nine months, a child is created in its mother's womb. She nurtures the seed so it can grow and in nine months life is born.

That analogy formed within my novel when I entered the last date and wrote the end closing out the last chapter of my book. It was my baby—my child, and I nurtured it every day by feeding it chapter after chapter, completing the immediate goals I had set for myself. My self-esteem was through the roof and it was the most ultimate high I ever felt in my life. On May 23, 2008, my vision became a reality. My book, Twist of Fate, was a finished piece of urban fiction. My book was born.

My next goal—buy a typewriter and type up the manuscript to get it publishing ready.

SUCCESS TIPS
What Does Each Tip Mean To You?

1. Add Value-________________________

2. Follow Your Passion-________________

3. Be Extraordinary-__________________

4. Start Now-________________________

5. Hunt for Good Mentors-______________

6. Build a Support Group-______________

7. Personally Know Your Finances-________

8. Get Help-________________________

9.	Learn Sales-________________________________

10.	Be Resilient-________________________________

EMOTION

(STEP THREE)

In this chapter, we will discuss emotions when being creative. We will also discuss the emotions we go through while following our dreams and creating our process.

EMOTION- strong feelings such as love, anger, or fear; emotional intensity or sensibility.

I am a very emotional person—it is both a gift and a curse within the lifestyle I live. However, it creates so much passion within my writing. When fans read my novels, they feel close to me. In the business that you chose you as an induvial will be passionate about it. That is one of the strongest emotions you will deal with when becoming successful. Sacrifices will be made; friends will be left behind for the greater good and you will always be in work mode to get it done. Be prepared to be emotional within your creative process.

You are at your best within the process when you are knowledgeable about the subject. That is where my passion lies within emotional fiction—I am an expert inside the genre because I created my own lane. I studied and read urban fiction plus many *How To* become a great writer book(s). The expertise came once my aspirations became bigger then writing a book. When I decided to start my own publishing company to help women and men incarcerated to share their stories is where the real work came in at. This is when I had to put these seven steps to work. Under pressure a diamond was born throughout several mistakes made and the perseverance of never giving up. Mindset is another important step towards success. What are your expectations of being successful? Explain it in depth. Write it down and tell it to yourself every day. This mindset will keep you motivated.

WHAT ARE YOUR EXPECTATIONS OF BEING SUCCESSFUL?

SUCCESS TIP

When you are stretched out in your bed in the wee hours in the morning, tossing and turning with your emotions tugging at you, GET UP! Share your feelings with the sun creeping over the horizon. WRITE DOWN YOUR THOUGHTS!

When you envision a concept, or a backdrop behind your name, jump up and write it down. It is not a fleeting thought that holds no substance; it is the dreams and desires of one's heart. The heartbeat of emotions that runs through you is what is needed to pour out your ideas. It is your make-up—your D.N.A that will make your success story not just a story but also an experience. Inspiration is anywhere and everywhere. Emotional moments can transpire in the blink of an eye. Subliminal messages can create these emotional moments that need to be recorded, not forgotten.

INSPIRATION- creative force or influence stimulating creativity; divine influence; on the writing of scripture; sudden brilliant idea.

Subliminal messages, such as an old song playing to the person sitting in the next room, can create a moment. A Bible passage or an inspiration quote can cause some friction, make you ponder on a thought, have mixed emotions, a teaching moment on the next idea on how to be the next success story.

SUCCESS TIP

Everyone's process is different, but the one thing we all have in common when it comes to being successful is perseverance. Today, I challenge you to be as creative within your success story as you can. What is your deepest secret you possess? Remember—everyone loves reality, hope, and the reason WHY you had to do what you had to do to become successful! It is the thought that counts. However, to write it down makes it tangible. "I Will Be Successful!" Speak it into existence.

Subliminal messages come in all different forms, shapes, sizes, people, places, and things. You will need support and funds to help you complete certain goals. Supporters and people who have similar goals will help you fund your endeavors. All help is great thing and the best advice is given from the horse's mouth. One thing is for sure, and I cannot stress this enough, as humans, we all have emotions in common. That is where you want to draw from—your personal dreams, your fantasies, and the passion you feel about your success story. When someone can feel your passion surrounding your ideas, they will want to support you. People really don't know how much money is invested off of a hunch. Just remember, that hunch was fueled by passion.

SUCCESS TIP

If you pay attention, you will notice that you make time for the things that are high priority on your life list first. You make time to work, to pay the bills, you make time to eat, to have energy, you make time to spend with your loved ones, you make time to pay that car insurance, you make time to work out, and so on. Make time for your definition of SUCCESS.

YOU MUST MAKE TIME TO INVEST IN YOURSELF! YOUR DREAMS & YOUR

GOALS ARE PRIORITY TOO! MAKE THE TIME TO WORK FOR YOU! WAKE UP AN HOUR EARLY, BEFORE YOU GET READY FOR WORK, AND INVEST IN YOU! THAT WASTED TIME YOU GIVE SOCIAL MEDIA--INVEST IT IN YOU! EVERY SECOND OF THE DAY COUNTS IN YOUR LIFE.

#YOURGOALSARELIFE

DOUBT- uncertainty; undecided state of mind; skepticism; feel uncertain or undecided about; call in question.

****SUCCESS TIP****

This is the most common emotion anyone trying to break through has. _Break through what?_ I bet that is what you are asking yourself right now. What I mean by _break through_ is breaking through that mental block after you have started to build your brand, and nothing is pulling together. This usually happens in the middle of your process. The manifestation of a mental block strikes fears inside of you, insisting you cannot finish the process that you started to be successful. It nags you like your mother, telling you that you do not have the potential or the means to finish what you have started. Your ideas are roaming around; the money you need to invest is not adding up, will anyone support me when its time and the list goes on and on. These are the thoughts going through your mind, hitting the panic button.

A mental block is a mind thing and doubt plays a big part in the double feature. Now, on top of everything else, you are dealing with the doubt of 'Will anyone believe in you once your goal has been completed?' 'Will anyone have interest in what you have to offer to the world?' Well, you must finish what you have started and by all means necessary, finish the marathon to find out. In that moment when you want to give up is when you must keep going. You must keep running the marathon until the race is complete.

SUCCESS TIP

To get results you must take chances. Know your self-worth, no matter how much you doubt yourself. Doubt and negativity will come in many forms as you are reaching your potential. Life will also show up and show out, creating long lists of duties that can detour you from your goals. However, when you detour, just remember to handle the life event thrown at you…grow and learn from it and then get back to business.

**COURAGE-** the ability to disregard fear; bravery.

Find the courage within yourself to finish what you have started and identify it with your emotions. Have the courage to work through all trials and tribulations when life shows up; it is therapeutic.

Creativity is a healing tool for the soul. Have the courage to work through the pain, drawing from your life experiences and those around you. Find the courage to work when you do not feel like it.

LIFE HAPPENS

When I came home from prison my life was pulled in so many different directions. My dreams and my success plan were quickly put on the backburner as I tried to find a job, while spending time with my family. That does not even include the new relationship I had jumped in or the groups I had to attend. The bad habits I once again picked up quickly faded my book dreams to black.

It took four years and three life-changing events for me to believe in myself, to put my goals and plan into effect until my book was published. I needed something to feel good about as a person, to bring me back to life. Twist of Fate did not just save my life once—it saved my life twice. It gave me the hope that I needed to get me through the most trying times in 2015. This is what I mean when I tell you that emotions can heal the soul from the inside out and make you move mountains to become successful. The summer of 2014 was the worst; it brought death knocking at my front door. Three people I was in love with at one time or another in my life died one month after each other.

On June 25, 2014, I said goodbye to my ex-girlfriend as she closed her eyes for the last time at the age of forty-one. It was not the same type of hurt as losing a parent, and I know this because I lost my father when I was fifteen years old. Losing someone I once was in love with was totally confusing to my heart. It took something completely different out of me. My son had just yelled at me for not going to see her and when she ended up in the hospital, I was the last to arrive to see her off. In my mind, going to see her did not exist. I never thought it was that serious and I thought she would make it through, but when I heard the hurt in my son's voice, I lost my breath and choked on my tears. By the time I got to the hospital, I had missed the goodbyes and I was not able to sit in the room with her and hold her hand. My body hurt all over and my heart was broken.

Even though we were not on the best of terms, I never thought in a million years she would die. She was only forty-one years old and our sons still needed her. I could not look my son in the eyes from the hurt he possessed. The only thing I could think about was how selfish I had been. I made her illness all about me and how I felt, forgetting to be there for my son, who loved her very much, despite our nasty break up. Being a person who was comfortable with self-medication I began to hit the bottom of the drinking glass hard.

On August 16, 2014, I received a phone call from a friend, informing me that someone very special to me was murdered. At that point in my life she was more than just a friend, she was the one who was honest with me about being who I was.

She helped me understand that I would have to transition and grow up if I wanted to be blessed. I will always remember the last conversation we had because it was about just that—life, growth, and the love we shared. She will continue to be my guardian angel.

My friend was killed by a pair of hands she knew. Life has a funny way of showing up and kicking us where the sun doesn't shine. She was buried in a shallow grave at the end of the struggle, taking her last breath at the hands of someone who claimed they loved her. I am not going to take anything from him because as you can see, he loved her to death. In my opinion, I just wish he had loved himself enough not to be so selfish. The hurt and the pain from her loss was real, it took over my rational thinking while my bottomless drinking glass remained filled.

One month later, I stood with her family once again, only this time it was to bury her father, who had died from a broken heart. Her tragic death left a stain on his heart that could not be lifted. His little girl being murdered killed his will to live, meanwhile, I fell in love with her ghost. By the time it was all said and done, I had to undergo therapy to get back on track. This is what I mean when I say life happens and we must get up and keep pushing.

LIFE TIP

You do not have to go to church to know your God of understanding and the person reading your story can be reading the only bible they will ever know. Every success story has a beginning, a struggle and how they made it to the top (The happy ending) … #ContinueToGrind

While in therapy I finally got the courage to believe in myself, to publish my novel I had been sitting on for eight years. While in-group I was listening to everyone's introductions when I realized it was time to tell my story, to start healing.

It became my motivation to see something good in myself once again.

Twist of Fate brought me back to life! I began to work double-time on the small goals I needed to complete for my publishing process. It was time for me to Be My Own Boss.

I invested in as many overtime hours as I needed to fund myself financially. I worked non-stop until the book was published on January 22, 2016. To see what I created in my hands from cover to cover was the best feeling I had ever had in my life. It was the ultimate high. As the tears ran down my face, I realized that I had done it, despite everything life had brought me through. These brief moments I have shared with you is not even the half of what I have been through, but I am here and I am a self-published author. I own my own publishing rights and a Publishing Company called Emotional Fiction Publishing Firm.

Life happens but you must keep on pushing. It took four and a half years for me to get it together and publish a manuscript I had been sitting on for a long time. There isn't any right or wrong way to do things when you're trying to reach your goals. It's about the 'do' process and finding the boss in you, just as I found the boss in me.

ENERGY

(STEP FOUR)

ENERGY- capacity for activity; force; vigor.

You need energy to fuel the ambition, to reach the destination of your goals, and to thrive off the emotional depth you need when in process of completing your goals to be successful. Energy and the will to do be the best at what you do is rooted within your being. *YOU*, must turn that power on and crank up the gear shift to get in 'do' mode.

WILL- faculty by which a person decides what to do; strong desire or intention; determination; willpower.

Your ability to will yourself out of bed every day is a start. Now, make sure you will yourself into walking into your purpose.

Ambition is merely will in disguise and it is necessary. You always must have a dream or a vision to stay focused and determined. Stay one hundred percent positive in any situation—it will keep you on your toes. I know you are asking yourself 'How can you do that with so many different negative things going on around you?' How you think strongly influences how you behave, the choices you make, how you conduct yourself and how you live your life. When you stand with beings that are doing something different, it allows you to see and hear different ideas and strategies for how to be successful.

I surround myself with winners, people who have made it to the next level in their journey.

These people gave me advice on how they became successful, how they failed and overcame rejection. The best part of shadowing a mentor is, you can observe them in other roles that they play to see how they work the crowd. Now, you have the inside track on how to present your ideas in a room filled with people who know more then you. Surrounded by negative thoughts and feelings you will begin to feel the same as your surroundings. If you are around someone every day that complains about what they do not have, what is not being done for them and how it is not their fault when nothing goes right, you begin to do the same. You start to wake up and find ways to cop out of giving life your best shot for today. You begin to pick up on others' pain and start taking on their burdens without even knowing it.

At this time in your process you must have people around you with the same goals. You want people around you that hustle just as hard as you do, and you want people to look at you for motivation.

Positive energy is needed to generate more positive energy within. It is the law of attraction, when you know better, do better, and you cannot say I did not tell you. I live by this energy, meditating to grasp ahold of the positivity within. My days are a lot better as of today because I dwell on positive vibes and what I can do to become a better person in the moment. Taking it day by day I created small personal goals to maintain my thinking. I also created small writing and reading goals to become goal oriented. Once you begin to set your specific success goals and they reach their destination, your self-confidence begins to climb. You become confident with what is expected of you, as a successful leader and you are comfortable with your expectations, even when life throws you a curve ball. With self-confidence comes the energy that was there all along, lying dormant.

It is amazing what you can do when you put your mind to it. What is even more fantastic is how your body follows behind your thoughts. Anything you focus on in life will become bigger when you have the right mindset. Your ambition makes you follow suit with your emotions, your will and your intellect generate that self-sufficient energy you need to find the determination in you.

MOTIVATION- the general desire or willingness of someone to do something.

Energy and motivation keep us pushing, pushing all forces to work together. I cannot say all good energy that will get those juices flowing. Negative energy can often push you a lot harder. Yes, ***YOUR*** negative energy can be a useful tool.

The negative energy thrown at you (you will never make it, you're not a good at anything, why are you wasting your time?) will give you the motivation to prove them wrong when you have a strong mindset. Doubt can be a good friend or a mean enemy. Seeing negativity all around you can make you want something different out of life when you recognize the risk. These eye-opening experiences will help make you stay focus and on the right path to achieving the goals to become successful.

The spirit of a man will sustain his infirmity; but a wounded spirit who can bear?
Proverbs: 18:14

This means that regardless of what comes into a person's life, he or she can bear up under it. A strong spirit within will sustain those times of trouble. If the spirit is weak or wounded, you will have a hard time bearing anything in life. What doesn't kill us will make us stronger. Fight for what you want.

Keep people around you who are doing what you are doing. Sit with winners and I guarantee you the conversation will be different. Put yourself in situations with people who have accomplished what you are trying to do. Stand next to the encourager, the exhorter; the positive energy rubs off. Good ideas are spoken into existence. When you think it, you speak it, and eventually you become the energy source in your own life, much like the sun gives the world light.

You teach from your learning experiences; you build up and speak life into others with flourishing words of wisdom through your story. This is a part of you and your opinions as your eyes see fit. You are the superabundance, a testimony to others in your field once you have accomplished STEPS 1, 2 and 3. Walking into your purpose is an eye-opening experience.

It is positive energy, negative energy, its music, circumstances, and a love story that possesses the lust, the cunning metaphors and the driven face of determination.

I starred, directed and produced the first ten chapters of my book on pure negative adrenalin, mad at the world and the decisions I had made. Overall, I had something to prove to the world and myself.

When I was dealing on the streets of Pittsburgh PA, I had one goal and one goal only—to get at a dollar. Even though I was in a negative state of mind, I was very goal oriented and I set goals for myself every day, according to the streets. Those that have been in my shoes…you know what those goals consist of. For twelve years of my life I woke up at the crack of dawn to sell poison in my community. I made money from the broken spirits of women, men and children too. I thrived from their misery by possessing materialistic things to make me feel good about myself.

I was a dealer, but I was the mother of a child as well. My son grew up watching me, and all the negativity surrounding my so-called life. Being an alcoholic, one thing I never did was judge. We were all out there chasing something. No matter what, I loved the streets and the code of ethics that came along with it. I fell in love with the lust, the temptations, and the worldly possessions. I loved being my own boss and doing whatever the heck I wanted to do.

I have heard that as a hustler, you should be feared rather than loved, but my code of ethics proved that wrong. I was never a gun totter, I never sold any fake drugs, I did not take advantage of the sick, and the love I showed was returned to anybody who spent a dollar with me. I fed many who were hungry and gave the shoes and shirts right off my back. I gave out Christmas cards just to show my appreciation. When I say I loved the hustle and I loved the game, I really did. The same people that I tried to help make money, the ones I made sure were eating and drinking, or gave a place to stay, etc.—they were the same ones to let me down when I needed them the most.

My so-called friends called me a snitch after I plead guilty to a five to ten-year plea. No one sent any money orders, came to visit, or sent any letters. The only people who supported me when I was down were my family and I love each of them for being there for me.

In my cell I sat, beyond angry, hurt and heartbroken. The more I sat alone with my own thoughts the more I began to hate everything the streets stood for. Once the withdrawal from the alcohol kicked in, I began to hate myself. With my life hanging in the balance and a pen in my hand I wrote and wrote and wrote. Every character was a different part of me—the good, the bad, and the ugly. Twist of Fate is full of ugliness, my truth, my therapy, and I love it. Find your truth. Find that hidden talent. God blessed each of us with something great.

The negative energy fueled my good intentions and at that time, I did not even know it. I had no clue. I used the negative energy, the ugliness I had seen and heard in my world, every derogatory statement I thought about myself and I took it out on the pen and paper. I was all over the place when I tapped into that energy. I was writing poems, treatments for other books and random ideas. I made sure I took time out once a day for each idea, but I made sure my novel was my priority until it was complete. If you do not have any order within setting your goals you will have many unfinished projects. We do not want that! Stay focused!

Doubtful situations are very common when trying to create your own lane. Even with all the doubt, continue to study and be proactive within your goals. Let the negative energy fuel you and allow you to prove to yourself and others your self-worth. Take all the negative energy and create a positive force.

Write your ideas down, read your ideas and speak them into existence, and always set goals to get through the day. Use that negative thinking in a positive light. If you can get up at the ass crack of dawn to do a negative deed or wait in line for the next tennis shoe to drop, you can get out of bed to educate yourself and work towards your goals.

Treat each goal you set as a move you must make to stay alive.

Use all energy to your advantage and focus on the ***How-To*** aspect (How to be successful).

What makes you unique? When you find the answer to that question and factor that into your determination plan, you will be unstoppable.

****SUCCESS TIP****

Draw from your own friends and family, as well as your personal experiences.

Thrive off the solar system of energy, which is the positive and negative energy.

Fall in love with your emotions, both positive and negative, to create your next plan.

Use the energy and the vibe of others around you. We are our own worst enemy at times.

You can do this! Exercising your ability to become something great is just as easy as riding a bike. You remember how hard it was to ride when the training wheels first came off? However, over time the ride began to get easier and easier the more you practiced. Give yourself a chance before counting yourself out!!! NOW LET'S GO!!! GET TO WORK!!!

DETERMINATION

(STEP FIVE)

DETERMINATION- 1. Firmness of purpose; resoluteness: 2. the process of establishing something exactly by calculation or research: 3. the controlling or deciding of something's nature or outcome: 4. the cessation of an estate or interest: 5. a tendency to move in a fixed direction.

PLAN- 1. a detailed proposal for doing or achieving something: 2. an intention or decision about what one is going to do: 3. decide on and arrange in advance: 4. design or make a plan of (something to be made or built):

Your determination is like a muscle you must put to work! You must exercise the muscle so that it can become stronger. That is what you do with any other muscle within your body structure. You work that muscle until you are controlling nature's outcome. You work it out until it is strong enough to thrive on its own and you are winning. Your ambition has you in place to make your next move. The passion wrapped up in your emotions are in full throttle awaiting to start the process and your energy is at an all-time high to see results. Being determined has set everything in motion from the beginning and will get you to the end of the process you have set in place. Create your definition for the phrase; determination plan based off the dictionary definition and what is in your heart.

DETERMINATION PLAN-

____

____

____

____

____

____

____

____

____

SUCCESS TIPS

Create a list of descriptive words for the idea you are working on and use them to create 30 second presentations to pitch when you see a potential client or investor. This is called the elevator pitch. To be honest with you, as adults our attention span is 30 seconds flat. If you do not woo us in by then our minds are looking past you and your idea.

Take all your emotions and feeling and write them out within your spill. Remember, you have 30 seconds! Make every second count! I sit right now, as we speak, writing my truth to help the next person become great. Yes! I am talking to you and everyone else reading this book right now. Contribute your wisdom! Don't be selfish!! The greatest success story often suffered the most before the breakthrough.

When you were a child this was something easy to do. You exercised this part of your brain a lot more when you were eight or nine. You created full-page dialogues for those Barbie's sitting poolside, and let us not forget about those wrestling men hanging out on the steel cage. It was easy to use your imagination at that age, planning out the dreams for your life and acting them out in stages. You must go back and find that inner child inside of you. Make him/her grow up to entertain a new social group of Barbie's and wrestling men. This time, however, you are creating full dialogues to fit into your idea of becoming successful. From creative ideas, to graphic monstrous details, you must be ready to entertain the marketable audience. Everyone always needs help with something. If you can find a way to help someone and make money while doing it, you are in there.

Writing your 30 second elevator tips to strengthen your introduction skills will help you. It will help you in creating different approaches for different people. No one person is a like, and all social groups are different when it comes to the approach. You must be able to engage in conversation and know what introduction to use when approaching certain people and groups. This can also give you direction and allow you to see what you need to work on within developing your marketing tools. Remember—you are only as good as your imagination. Let it run free and wild.

<u>CREATIVITY-</u> the use of imagination or original ideas, especially in the production of an artistic work.

Creativity is a source of positive energy and preparing from this ingenious place creates a positive flow of planning. Creativity is the forefront of the success process and without creative conceptions you have nothing to articulate. Recent studies I have researched for this project have confirmed creativity comes from a deep emotional connection within us. Creativity and imagination go hand and hand. Your imaginative thinking is broken down into two parts. Let us discuss them.

Primary Imagination: this comes from your unconscious and it is the source of all new ideas and insights. It is where your inspiration lies, where the inspiration comes from, making up only 10 percent of the creative process.

Secondary Imagination: this is the 90 percent that involves editing, discipline, logic, structure, and order. Creativity includes both inspiration and preparation. When creating a determination plan you need to discover how to combine the primary and secondary creativity process to be a creative master.

<u>EXAMPLE</u>

For an automobile to run smoothly all parts must work together. If the engine locks, a tire goes flat or if you run out of gas the car will not run. Each part depends on the other to run and to run successfully.

While developing a determination plan recognize each aspect of its process. Stay on point with each aspect of your craft. You will always need to have a direction to get you to the finish line—your destination. To be more creative means having the courage to return to a time when your self-consciousness was free, allowing that spontaneously creative side of you to emerge through.

Create your own blueprint after researching your craft. Let the rest of the judgmental fools catch up. Do not worry about what the next person is saying. Remember, many have failed before becoming great. Never stop your success process, create your own constricted formula, and always allow that imagination to run wild and free.

SUCCESS TIP

Record your thoughts, feelings, ideas and even your dreams. Get into the habit of journaling your daily routines. This will allow you to go back to see what has worked and not worked out for you.

When you are putting together your determination plan you want to get your creative juices flowing and get those ideas down.

Think without censoring your thoughts, feelings, or ideas. Do not ask yourself, 'Is it good'.

Just continue with your plan to get as much information down at that time.

It does not have to be right at the moment just tangible evidence that you can see, read and touch.

UNDER CONSTRUCTION

(STEP SIX)

Do you know why you want to successful?

Do you want to make a lot of money?

Do you want to be famous?

Do you want to get recognition?

Do you want to entertain others?

Do you want to be your own boss?

Do you want to become a brand?

Do you want to be a public speaker?

It is important to look at the motives for wanting to be your own boss. Only one percent of the world will be millionaires' studies have said. If the motives are not strong enough, you probably will not finish what you started. I had something to prove to myself and to others who watched me sell poison in my community for years. It is imperative that I help the community that I had taken life from. I believed my story could show other convicted felons that it is never too late to make a change. I believe that everyone can change their life if they want to. Through my struggles and beliefs, I write to help the writers like me.

However, maybe you need to shed some light about a specific matter with others. Perhaps you want to tell people about your strong opinions and beliefs through your freedom of expression. Can you be in dire need to tell your personal story? If deep down inside all you can think about is your idea, that you can't live without watering the talent that God gave you, then pursue your dream and don't stop until the world knows your name.

SUCCESS TIP

If you have no idea about an idea you want to pursue, <u>PLEASE DO YOUR RESEARCH BEFORE YOU START INVESTING MONEY & TIME.</u> If you do not follow this rule in everything you do, your determination plans will flat line with no resuscitation.

The days when you do not feel like grinding, grind anyway! They will always be your most creative days.

Always make time to nurture your talent. God gave you a purpose, so experiment and find it!

Whatever you want to present to the world, always bring your passion, your core values, and your beliefs within your plans. I draw everything I write from personal experience…that's my trademark, my writing secret. That is emotional fiction. When invested personally and emotionally your clients will also be invested personally and emotionally in the storyline and with your ideas.

To be a good success story you must have the courage to expose yourself, the ugly truth, and the risk of being vulnerable. It worked for me. Drawing from personal situations and educating others on how you came through can help the next person find their way.

The success factor is not just about goals, writing and reading, it is about becoming a boss and finding the boss strategy within you. It took me awhile, but I have found mine.

Most urban fiction writers are self-published, started with self-publishing, or created the avenue for us—the new and up-coming self-publishers. Our urban youth 'do read' and so do black people. At one point in time people said, we did not read books, and then the next thing you know, more and more black literature started popping up all over the Internet.

Vickie Stringer, the CEO of Triple Crown Publishing did it the best in my opinion, dropping ten novels and creating a brand. She is the founder of Triple Crown Publishing, which has published dozens of books and brought a lot of authors to life.

Shannon Holmes, by producing such lofty sales numbers, was able to parlay the success of his first novel into a two book, six figure deal, with publishing giant, Simon & Schuster. He achieved his initial success with his first novel, B-more Careful, which sold a half a million copies within one year.

Do not let anybody tell you there is not. This man started writing in a jail cell and signed his first literary contract from prison, while serving a five-year sentence for various drug convictions. That is truly an amazing feat when you consider that Holmes had never even written a short story in his life. He honestly made the best of a bad situation.

When I started writing my first novel, I did not have a format or an agenda, I just knew I had something to say and I needed to get it out. When I read about Shannon Holmes and Vickie Stringer it opened my eyes to a whole new way of living. I still have the article I read of them from Jet Magazine. It went from hanging on my closet door in prison to sitting in a frame on my desk in my office.

The writing process of my first novel was my therapeutic journey. It was the only thing I had control over, as the state told me what to do majority of the time. While I sat in my cell, I schemed on what I could come up with next. When you open my book to the first chapter, what I give you is a piece of me. I started in a prison cell and now I am here teaching you. The steps are doable if you are willing to do the work. You can become a writer, a rapper, run your own business, be a star athlete or a preacher. Remember, these steps can be used in any success story you want to create. I have created several opening up my own Publishing

Company and Travel Agency. Following these steps, I am up two business and I change the forecast when it is not sunny in my hometown.

SUCCESS TIP

Remember... your story can help thousands recover from their storm. YOU can become a life coach by building from your own life experiences. Push yourself and use your determination plan to be as successful as need be to your definition of success.

#SuccessComesFromHardWork

CONSTRUCTIVE CRITICISM- criticism or advice that is useful and intended to help or improve something, often with an offer of possible solutions.

You must be able to take constructive criticism. You also must know what that is as well.

Constructive criticism is different from people just being dicks, so know the difference and make people respect you and your ideas when giving their opinions. People will use constructive criticism to try to undermine what it is you are trying to do—know the difference, believe in yourself, and give yourself the chance to be great.

My advice to everyone who reads these quick tips is that you Google and research more learning tools to help you along the way—to help you become successful in whatever adventure your heart desires. This is the most constructive criticism you are going to get from me.

"As human beings we love drama sugar coated with a dash of reality."
Nikki Flowers

Be Your Own Boss

- The goal to success is never giving up on your dreams.

- Part of being successful is believing in yourself enough to invest in yourself. Learn the business and recognize when you need help.

- Do not be afraid to invest in others to improve the wealth of your independent projects. Create a business plan and keep it on you at all times. You never know who you are going to run into that will hear your journey and want to invest. Remember, there are many ways a person can invest in you. Do not always be hung up on money. Knowledge is just as good as gold and you have it for a lifetime.

- Always research on the Internet. Make Google your new best friend and research everything. A simple question placed into the Google search engine can educate you on grants (free money), small business loans, how to create a grant and how to repair your credit, allowing you to invest in yourself.

- Networking is the next key to your success. It also plays a big part in your success. You have three big social media sites to create a platform on and many more to blend into to shine light on your projects.

FACEBOOK: Facebook is a popular website that allows registered users to create profiles, upload photos and videos, send messages, and keep in touch with friends, family and colleagues. The site, which is available in 37 different languages, includes public features such as:

- Marketplace - allows members to post, read and respond to classified ads.
- Groups - allows members who have common interests to find one another and interact.

- Events - allows members to publicize an event, invite guests, and track who plans to attend.

- Pages - allows members to create and promote a public page built around a specific topic.

- Presence technology - allows members to see which contacts are online and chat.

Within each member's personal profile, there are several key networking components. The most popular is arguably 'the wall', which is essentially a virtual bulletin board. Messages left on a member's wall can be text, video or photos.

Another popular component is the virtual photo album. Photos can be uploaded from the desktop or directly from a smartphone camera. There are no limitations on quantity, but Facebook staff will remove inappropriate or copyrighted images. An interactive album feature allows the member's contacts, who are generically called 'friends', to comment on one another's photos and identify, or tag, people in the photos.

Another popular profile component is status updates, a <u>microblogging</u> feature that allows members to broadcast short Twitter-like announcements to their friends. All interactions are published in a news feed, which is distributed in real-time to the member's friends.

TWITTER: Twitter employs a purposeful message size restriction to keep things scan-friendly. In the case of Twitter, every microblog 'tweet' entry is limited to 280 characters or less. Great!!! When you are promoting you want to keep your post to a word minimum and catchy. Posting on Twitter will give you practice on how to promote with hashtags and a catchy rhythm, using only 280 characters. This size cap promotes the focused and clever use of language, which makes tweets very easy to read, but very challenging to write. This size restriction has really made Twitter a popular social tool and a great way to promote to the stars.

Create accounts as soon as possible for your strictly for your business vendor. Keep them separate from your personal page but link all the accounts together. When you do this, you make one post on a social media site, and then you can tag in all three sites. Different socialites are on each site, so it creates a bigger networking platform. By having all three social media sites linked to one another you can reach several thousand different people, companies, and talent scouts. It is important to let your fans into your reality.

INSTAGRAM: Instagram is made for sharing photos and videos from a smartphone. This app brought the hashtag to life, which we will touch on momentarily. To hashtag the correct topic under your picture or video that you post can create a huge buzz. By doing so you also have the potential to go viral.

Similar to <u>Facebook</u> or <u>Twitter</u>, everyone who creates an Instagram account has a profile and a news feed. When you post a photo or video on Instagram, it will be displayed on your profile. Other users who follow you will see your posts in their own feed. Likewise, you will see posts from other users whom you choose to follow. Once again, with the hashtag and trending topics you can view many profiles without being followed or following a person.

Pretty straight forward, right? It is like a simplified version of Facebook, with an emphasis on mobile use and visual sharing. Just like other social networks, you can interact with other users on Instagram by following them, being followed by them, commenting, hitting the like button, tagging, and private messaging.

<u>HASHTAGS-</u> are key words, which can be used to organize messages on social media sites. They allow viewers who are not in your circle to see your brand, which is key to networking. This then facilitates the searching and grouping of messages with hashtags. Hashtags are preceded by the pound sign (#) and can be a word or a short phase. As you have seen in some of my success tips, I used the hashtag.

I have a Facebook page to promote my books, my publishing company, and my travel agency. I pulled a lot of my coaching tips from my pages, so make sure to follow me and catch me if you can keep up.

The hashtag creates a platform that anyone can see. A person does not have to be your friend in order to see what you posted; you can simply share the same interest in a hobby, inspiration, what is trending and so on. The hashtag is a great avenue to get recognition and build a following with people all over the word who share the same ideas and beliefs that you do.

#Hashtags #HashtagsToPromote

REALITY TV- Reality television is the biggest form of exposing your brand, so get ready to shoot a lot of footage to create a YouTube channel. This is another big networking tool and you can collect royalties when you get popular enough.

Always remain in a positive light. Your image is everything from the moment you are thinking about creating a brand until the finished product is produced. Your brand, your-self, your social media platforms, and your business are a brand—an image.

Getting to know people in your lane can help you expand your brand, teaching you how to move within your investment, what you need money for and how it should be spent. This success formula is a complete module of what needs to be done to become successful within any idea you chose if you are passionate about it.

What does success mean to you? The definition of success, according to Webster's Dictionary, is the accomplishment of an aim or purpose. But what is the definition of success that *you* have for *your* ideas, goals and beliefs? You wrote a definition in the previous chapter. Write another one and compare your definitions. We want to see if your thinking pattern has changed after reading the steps.

Success-

Write it down, review the definitions, memorize them and always focus on bringing the definitions to life. It will be ever-changing as you begin to grow, accomplish your goals, and create new goals to achieve.

You must be prepared when you want people to invest in you and your brand. In the end, you must be ready to invest in yourself. When approaching a person of interest, a nonprofit organization, or your home church or institution for support and funding always be knowledgeable and confident of your product and business plan. Always have a plan and a goal in mind. The way you speak to others, carry yourself, and answer direct questions under pressure will get you into a lot of doors with no money. Create an opportunity for you to become successful. If you do not invest in, YOU nobody else will! Be your own boss!!!

THE CONCLUSION

(STEP SEVEN)

Everyone's favorite question to ask me is this––How did you go about getting your book published? How did you start a publishing company? Wow, how did you start two companies?

Honestly, I did not have a clue on what to do or how to do it back then. I just knew it had to be done. My first novel, Twist of Fate: A Truth Wrapped In A Beautiful Lie, is over 10 years old.

When I came home to the halfway house in 2011 to complete my last year of a 5-year sentence, all I had was a dream. I had a dream of being on Oprah's show, being published by Triple Crown Publishing and blowing up like Shannon Holmes, Vickie Stringer, and Terri Woods. After going through my trials and tribulations and finding the boss in me I took these short, easy steps to start my success story. Believe me when I say, I made lots of mistakes before getting it right. To this day, I still have not published the perfect novel. I am almost there though…just wait on it. In the end I had to go through everything I went through for me to get to this very moment. Trust me; I spent lots of money through trial and error, learning the process I am sharing with you. This is what it all boils down to.

<u>STEP ONE:</u>

Prepare! Prepare! Prepare! When you feel like it and when you do not feel like it, prepare anyway.

The only way you will know if you can do it is if you finish what you start. Without a finished determination plan you cannot get started.

STEP TWO:

Step Two is my favorite. Success Stories are not written. They are rewritten and often changed multiple times within the success process until perfection is achieved. This is okay and a must. You may have to find different approaches to bring your dream to life. Just because one theory did not work does not mean the next theory will not. Make the necessary changes you need until your plan is running successfully. There are many factors that go into becoming success in both your professional and personal life but the one factor that is required is taking action. Most people miss out on reaching their full potential because they never start. They are always preparing, planning and waiting for the best time to start. If I waited until I was ready, I would not have a coaching practice, a website, a blog, a workshop, etc. The stars rarely align, and you will never be completely ready so just start now and adjust along the way. Are you waiting for something before you start? What is really the worst thing that could happen if you got started right now? If you are someone that has just been waiting, after reading this get started on what you have wanted to do.

STEP THREE:

Step three is the most important step of them all. Creating a determination plan using all the steps provided in the book. Following these steps provided in the book will give you the ambition, the emotion, the energy and the confidence to pull this thing off. When you can see everything mapped out within the plan and the small goals being accomplished it gives you the courage to succeed. Your well-oiled machine is working. Things rarely work out the way you planned and there will always be distractions and stumbling blocks that you must deal with when you are on your road to success. The key point to remember is to persist and to develop the courage to move on even when everyone around you is telling you it is ok to give up. This does not mean stubbornly holding on to your original plan but rather continuing to pursue your goal as long as the reasons for doing so is still valid (Make sure you know the "Why" of what you want). When everything seems to be going wrong, keep in mind that "the road to success is paved with a thousand failures" so each failure brings you closer to where you want to be.

<u>STEP FOUR:</u>

Step four is *The Push*—something that we all need after our success plan and our idea is ready to go. Now, you are ready to get started on taking over the world. However, at that very moment of glory the doubt begins to set in. Do I have the money to invest in myself? What if people don't like it? What if I don't make any money?

With these questions arising, the doubt sets in and these thoughts start to become overwhelming and scary. It's during that very moment that you begin looking for a way out, finding other ways to spend the money that are more important because you are afraid to invest in yourself. Thoughts such as, 'Let me pay these last few bills off so I can focus on my success plan.' 'I didn't know marketing packages were this costly. I'll just wait until I get my taxes.' 'What if I invest all this money and I don't make it?'

STOP RIGHT THERE! You will never know the answer to any of those questions running through your head if you do not invest in yourself. You must push yourself and believe in yourself. It is okay to make mistakes because that is how we learn. In fact, I put a few of my own learning experiences in here to show you that it is okay. It is okay to be human. To let you in on a big secret—I did not make thousands of dollars or sell thousands of books coming out of the starting gate. In fact, many entrepreneurs do not make any money off their first invention until the second or third great idea factor has come along. So, make sure to give yourself a pat on the back and a round of applause for finding the boss in you, which helped you get to this very moment.

The hard work is over; your first success story is complete. Give yourself a chance to fail so that you can succeed if need be. Hey, you could be the one to shock the world and break the Internet with your idea and become a millionaire. Continue to keep moving forward. Start researching all the components you need to make your dreams true.

STEP FIVE:

You must invest in yourself. No matter what, you must get the job done. If you do not know something, take the time out to research it in order to help yourself. Consider finding a mentor to help guide you through the process. Always remember, everyone who has made it had to start from somewhere. The hustle is to invest in yourself, working the overtime is to invest in yourself and waking up 4AM to write down today's goals is investing in yourself. When you do just that you will always stay ahead of the game, and no matter if you're self-publishing a novel or going to the studio to pay for your session you will succeed in all that you do.

<u>STEP SIX:</u>

No matter what you do and where you go, you cannot go wrong with adding value. Value is anything that people are willing to pay for. In your professional life, the more value you can offer the more money you can make. In your personal life, more value translates to closer relationships and strong personal growth. The best way to add value is to find the intersection between what people are willing to pay for and what service or product you can offer that is aligned with your values, strengths, and goals. How are you adding value to your employers and loved ones today? What can you do to increase your ability to add value? Be extraordinary… If you do the same thing as everyone else, it's hard to be successful. It is important to find the edge and then push past it. That is how you become noticed and get what you want. Whether it is money, meaningful relationships and/or a sense of personal accomplishment, the extraordinary person attracts them all. How are you extraordinary? If you feel just ordinary, what are you going to do to become extraordinary?

<u>STEP SEVEN:</u>

The last and final step is to create a list of everything you need to do to accomplish your goal. Even if you detour from the list, you must make sure that you find your way back!

Everything I have learned I have done on my own through trial and error and I have made it through. All the information I am sharing with you in this How-To guide I learned by the do process and research. The learning experiences are just that, but you must believe in yourself to invest in yourself so you can go through the growing process.

Going through the growing process will allow you to make it through the learning experiences. If I can do this, so can you! Follow the steps I have provided for you today and create your own lane, become your own boss. These steps are the laws of attraction. You can apply them to your everyday life and be your own boss. Instead of watching ratchet television, invest in you and use one of the

world's most powerful tools to educate yourself—
the Internet. Keep this little back pocketbook close
to you. When you need that extra push, *The Success
Factor* will be there to keep you focused, to keep
you believing in yourself, and to keep you investing
in you as a brand. NOW LET'S GET TO WORK!!

Be Your Own Boss

What More Can I Say

By: Mark Bunting 152196

It's pure, it has no boundaries, it's unexplainable, the essence is like a waterfall or a fountain, and sometimes it's conditional or maybe a tactic, all while being visualized as a game and the prey becomes the practice.

It's an intricate mixture of lies that's almost as complex as drawing one's complexion. Coming from multiple points of views it's described differently depending on one's perception—Who AM I???

I did six years upstate. I came home and tried to do the right thing for about a month and a half. Then, without warning, I quit my job and started busting moves. I met this chick whose skin looked like 'Keisha,' off of Belly. She was about 5'6 and 105 pounds; a petite chocolate thing. In this story, I will call her Shay. She sold weed but was struggling financially. I was doing good busting moves from her spot, so I paid all her bills, giving her what she asked for since she allowed me to do me within her space. I had three phones booming and I gave one to her for her work. Yeah, the bitch can hustle the big boy bags too, most definitely a turn on and I was gone off that thirty-two-year-old, signature cocoa brown, thick in all the right places single momma.

I was only twenty-six out there, trying to live the American dream. We went out to all different types of sports bars, paintballing, laser tag, Zone 28,

Kennywood, the movies, and dinner, all while having so much fun together. In the next breath, the Attorney General raided her crib and now she was turning state evidence on the kid—me.

I loved her unconditionally and I still do, even though she was telling on me as we speak. I couldn't believe it; I would've given her the shirt off of my back. It was then I realized she only loved me for her own personal gain. *Damn! Was it really love, or was I just the next come up, the next bust a move, or the next thing popping?*

As soon as we got locked up, I got her out of jail, leaving myself behind because a detainer was in place. Within a month of her being home she showed her true colors, turning the state's evidence on me. Because of this situation, it inspired me to write about a loveless encounter of betrayal. I was gone off her; I guess she didn't feel the same about me. Relationships are always like that—someone always loves harder than the other. I was used to being the puppet master. Now I know what it feels like being the puppet.

Other Books by Nikki Flowers

TWIST OF FATE

Egypt Winters was abandoned by her mother at birth. Raised by her God-fearing grandmother and fast-living aunt, Egypt eventually abandons them for the harsh streets of Pittsburgh. Turning her back on God, Egypt makes one bad choice after another until a single split decision leaves her in the hands of a sadistic, local drug dealer. She is held hostage by the one-time friend, raped and sold into sexual bondage.

While repeatedly force-fed heroin to keep her from escaping, she coasts through her life, past and present, searching for the answer to one question. How did she get to this point? She slowly connects the dots. An alcoholic by age sixteen, a drug addict for years after that, a street hustler and small-time dealer, a single mother whose father is brutally murdered, and a lesbian who rejects the one woman who loves her, Egypt's life is adrift.

Little does she know that the woman who gave her up at birth may yet bring her back to God. A twist of fate is knocking at the front door, and Egypt must decide whether to turn to hell's angel and end it all or find comfort from God and family she's come to hate.

*****

HUMBLE WATERS

Humble Waters was raised by a mother who paid homage to the struggle as a madam, her nightly kiss was missed. Her continued search for a nonexistent father, who was one of the most powerful men in the city of Pittsburgh, leads Humble to find real love cloaked in the father of her children, his dominant persona takes control of her life.

The seasons change and life is good until the only man she's ever known, is seized from her and sentenced to do hard time behind bars. Humble, the once faithful and devoted mother, falls victim to the boredom of her life as she tries to hold on to the memory of his touch. Saying yes to a night on the town leads her into the hands of the movers, the takers and the soul snatchers of the night.

Captivated by the flashing lights and introduced to the devil in the blink of an eye, one night turns into several. With the father of her children gone, the sheltered life he once provided, becomes nonexistent. Humble is introduced to the many hustles that are not visible to the naked eye and falls in love with adoration she discovers on the streets. A good girl gone bad creates a man who won't take no for an answer, a woman who can't walk away. A web of lies and deceit leave blood on Humble's hands.

About Nikki Flowers

Website: emotionalfictionpublications.com
Instagram: a_nikkiflowers_experience
Twitter: NikkiFlowers_1
Facebook:
facebook.com/EmotionalFictionPublishingHouse

You can contact Nikki Flowers at
emotionalfictionpublishing@gmail.com

Nikki Flowers is an inspiring writer who has breathed life back into street journalism. Writing with pure emotion from her heart, she has already penned many more novels that have yet to be released.

With her truth wrapped in a beautiful lie, she can tell a story that will keep you up late at night and into the wee hours of the morning. She invites you into these pieces of her world so that you can experience life through her eyes.

Raw and savvy, clear and uncut, street knowledgeable and educated, Nikki writes about the everyday lives of everyday people and will keep you in suspense with every word, every page, and every chapter. With a touch of class, a bit of wisdom, and a dose of harsh reality, she can make the words on a page come alive.

What reader could ask for anything more?